DESTROYING ETHNIC IDENTITY: THE KURDS OF TURKEY

**An Update
September 1990**

A Helsinki Watch Report

Human Rights Watch
485 Fifth Avenue
New York, NY 10017
Tel. (212) 972-8400
Fax (212) 972-0905

Human Rights Watch
1522 K Street, NW, #910
Washington, DC 20005
Tel. (202) 371-6592
Fax (202) 371-0124

ISBN 0-929692-63-2
Library of Congress Catalog Card Number: 90-71087

Table of Contents

Acknowledgments

This report is based largely on information gathered by Lois Whitman, Deputy Director of Helsinki Watch, and Eric Siesby, Chairman of the Danish Helsinki Committee, during a fact-finding mission to Turkey in May 1990. It was written by Lois Whitman. Portions of this report have appeared in the June 1990 Helsinki Watch newsletter *News from Turkey*.

Introduction

In early May, 1990, Helsinki Watch and the Danish Helsinki Committee sent a joint mission to Turkey to look into the situation of the Kurdish minority in southeastern Turkey and to investigate a recently-issued decree giving the regional governor broad powers to censor the press and to exile from the region people who present a "danger to law and order."[1] The mission met with lawyers, human rights activists, doctors, business people, journalists and villagers in Istanbul, Diyarbakir and Siirt. We were eager to see what changes had taken place in southeast Turkey since Helsinki Watch's visit in June of 1987 -- and, indeed, we found a number of changes, most, unfortunately, for the worse.

Most important, support among the Kurds for the PKK (the Kurdish Workers' Party, a separatist group waging guerrilla warfare against the Turkish government in the southeast) appeared to have grown a good deal. Turkish Parliamentarians and others from the southeast had told Helsinki Watch in June 1987 that a relatively small percent of Kurds supported the PKK; this time, however, leaders and others told us that, although the degree of support varied from place to place, most people now sympathized with the PKK because of the killings, harassment and abuse of Kurds by the security forces. The tactics used by the Turkish government appear to have been counterproductive -- to have driven more and more civilians into the arms of the PKK.

The police presence in the southeast is marked. The Helsinki mission was followed continuously. Our first meeting in a hotel in Diyarbakir with members of the local Human Rights Association was interrupted by a plain-clothes police officer who asked the head of the HRA how long the meeting would last, as he and his colleague wanted to leave to get some lunch. Unmarked police cars, usually containing four men, followed us out of Diyarbakir, turning back at the province line. A police car from Siirt took over later. No effort was made to conceal the surveillance. They claimed it was for our protection. As far as we could tell, the 1987 Helsinki Watch mission had not been followed.

---

[1] Participants in the mission were Lois Whitman, Deputy Director of Helsinki Watch, and Eric Siesby, Chairman of the Danish Helsinki Committee.

At roadblocks, our driver was questioned, but we were allowed to proceed. Local human rights activists and lawyers told us that local journalists and others unaccompanied by foreigners would not have been allowed to drive to Siirt, for example, without obtaining permission from the Regional Governor's office.

Police questioned people who had talked with us. On one occasion, a Kurd who had a casual street conversation with us was later picked up by police, questioned, and told not to associate with foreigners.

Local people told us of continual harassment by police. One businessman reported, for example, that when he and his family began a drive to a family wedding in Van, police stopped the car and questioned him for half an hour about the purpose of his trip. Others reported being followed regularly by police, and having their phones tapped. The Istanbul Human Rights Association reported in late 1989 that security forces cause great unrest in the southeast by stopping people on the roads and searching them.

Three weeks after our visit, three Scandinavian diplomats, Allen Christensen of Denmark, Irvin Hoyland of Norway, and Pino Valinoro of Finland, were detained in Diyarbakir for two and a half hours on the grounds that they had "carried out observations in the southeast without obtaining permission." The diplomats had repeated our trip; they had met with Zubeyir Aydar, head of the Siirt branch of the Human Rights Association, and others, and had visited evacuated villages.

The Kurdish community continues to be outraged by the Turkish government's denial of their ethnic identity. "We have no ethnic minorities," a "high official in Ankara" told Alan Cowell of *The New York Times* in February 1990. In May 1990, Ms. Fugan Ok, head of the human rights department of the Foreign Ministry, told Eric Siesby of the Danish Helsinki Committee that the Kurds are not a minority, since according to the Lausanne Treaty of 1923 only religious minorities are recognized. She also asserted that there is no discrimination against Kurds, but that such discrimination would exist if the Kurds insisted upon a separate language and a separate culture. Adnan Kahveci, Minister of Finance, also told Mr. Siesby in May that Kurds were not discriminated against, and that special Kurdish schools would create segregation and give rise to ethnic conflicts.

Kurds told us again and again that they want to be able to speak Kurdish officially, to read Kurdish books, to sing Kurdish songs,

2

to dance Kurdish dances, to celebrate Kurdish holidays, and to give their children Kurdish names. "We want the government to accept us as Kurds," one businessman told us, "and to leave us alone. We just want to be Kurds."

Guerrilla Warfare in the Southeast

Since 1984, Kurdish separatists have been waging guerrilla warfare in southeast Turkey.[2] About 2,000 people have been killed by the separatist PKK (Kurdish Workers' Party) and by government security forces since that time; 600 of these died in 1989, according to Regional Governor Hayri Kozakcioglu. According to *Middle East International* (June 22, 1990), 100 people were killed in the southeast in May 1990, and over 50 during the first half of June.

At least one third of the deaths in the southeast are of villagers, caught in the middle between the PKK and the security forces. PKK militants, for example, go to a village and demand food or other aid; if villagers refuse, they may be shot and killed by the PKK. If villagers comply, they may be detained, charged or killed by security forces.

PKK actions

No one knows exactly how may armed men carry out raids for the PKK; *The Washington Post* reported on June 1, 1990, that intelligence analysts estimate the number as 1,500 to 2,000, with another 1,500 along Turkey's borders or in training camps in the Bekaa Valley in Lebanon.

Although the PKK particularly targets village guards (villagers given arms by security forces and instructed to protect their villages from PKK terrorists), PKK fighters are reported to continue to shoot and kill other villagers as well, including women and children:

> o   On November 24 and 25, 1989, armed militants shot and killed 28 people, including 6 women and 13 children, in Ikikaya village in Hakkari's Yuksekova district. Eight were shepherds whom the group kidnapped and subsequently killed; a ninth shepherd escaped.

---

[2] See *Destroying Ethnic Identity: The Kurds of Turkey*, Helsinki Watch, March 1988.

5

o   On November 9, 1989, guerrillas raided a hamlet in
       Tunceli and shot to death 90-year-old Huseyin Ates in
       his house.

o   Guerrillas shot and killed former village headman Haci
       Aydinlik, his wife and three children, in the Silopi
       district of Mardin on February 26, 1990.

o   In mid-March the PKK abducted and killed nine
       employees of the state-owned Etibank's ferrochromium
       plant in Elazig; the group subsequently admitted
       responsibility for this act.

o   Six militants took a village primary school teacher
       from his house in the village of Cennetpinar in
       Kahramanmaras's Narli District and killed him on
       March 28, 1990.

o   On April 14, PKK militants attacked Bukardi village in
       Elazig, forced teachers and their wives out of the
       teachers' residence, and killed five people, including
       four teachers, with automatic weapons. (The PKK
       began targeting primary schools in November 1988,
       when they killed two teachers and set fire to three
       school buildings in villages in Mardin, Elazig and
       Tunceli. In the village of Yesilbelen in Elazig, the
       PKK group came in broad daylight, took the students
       and teacher out of the school building, sprinkled it with
       kerosene and set it on fire. The PKK then warned the
       villagers not to stay in the village.)

o   A group of guerrillas went to the home of grocery
       store owner Gevriye Bulut in Yemisli village in Mardin
       on May 1 and demanded food. When she resisted,
       they killed her and seriously wounded her husband and
       their two children.

o   On June 10, 1990, guerrillas reportedly killed 26
       villagers in a raid on Cevrimli village in Sirnak, north
       of the Syrian border. After a fight with village guards

defending the village, the rebels reportedly soaked four of the guards' houses with gasoline and set them on fire with their families inside. *(The Independent,* June 12, 1990.) The PKK has denied responsibility for the civilian deaths. The group claims that, after a fight between the PKK and village guards, PKK guerrillas left, and that security forces then entered the village and killed the villagers. As reporters have been denied access to the village, the facts of this massacre are unclear.

In an interview published in the daily *Hurriyet* on April 1, 1990, Abdullah Ocalan (known as Apo), the leader of the PKK, said that the fighting in southeastern Turkey could end if the Turkish government were willing to negotiate a truce with the group. Ocalan, whose headquarters are in the Bekaa Valley in Lebanon, said that the Kurds "can't secede from Turkey for the time being . . . for at least 40 years." He threatened that "a lot of blood will be spilled" if there is no ceasefire.

Government actions

The government has responded to the PKK with military action, evacuation of villages by giving inhabitants a choice of fighting the PKK or abandoning their homes, and by killing, detaining, torturing, imprisoning and harassing Kurds in the southeast.

Security forces vastly outnumber the guerrillas. According to *The Washington Post* (June 12, 1990), the Turkish military has 60,000 troops in the southeast; in addition, the regional governor controls 30,000 police and about 18,000 village guards and specially-trained police commandos.

Military actions against the guerrillas are carried out by the Turkish army, including "Special Operations Teams," as well as by police and gendarmes (internal security forces operating under the jurisdiction of the Ministry of the Interior). Interior Minister Abdulkadir Aksu reported in December of 1989 that since 1987, 5,837 individuals had been detained. He said that 3,574 of these had subsequently been freed, 1,989 arrested, and 283 kept under detention. He asserted that 322 terrorists had been killed during that period and 131 captured. *(Ankara Anatolia,* December 17, 1989.) Fighting seems to have intensified since that time; *Dateline* reported nine armed terrorists killed in Tunceli in early February, for example, seventeen in Savur and Nusaybin in mid-March, and 21 at Oymakkaya, near the Iraqi border, in early April.

Sometimes security forces kill villagers who they claim are "terrorists:"

o   On July 18 and 29, 1989, security forces in Hakkari shot and killed three men, Bunyamin Orhan, Sabri Orhan and Sehmus Orhan, whom they took to be members of the PKK. Other villagers, however, insisted that the three were innocent people, and that three other men from the village were missing and feared killed by security forces. According to an August 1989 issue of *Hurriyet Weekly*, Cumhur Keskin, an SHP deputy from the area, investigated the case and declared, "There has been no armed clash between the security forces and PKK members near the village of Yoncali. Those people who were described on television as PKK members are only inhabitants of the village. There are neither PKK members nor sympathizers in our village. Since 1984, the security of individuals in the area has been completely extirpated through these practices of the security forces."

o   In mid-September 1989, government forces killed as terrorists nine people in the Silopi district of Mardin. Five hundred local villagers carried out protest demonstrations, claiming that six of the nine were not PKK members at all. Police broke up the demonstration; 80 people were detained and five were beaten, including reporters from *Hurriyet* and *Milliyet*. On May 8, 1990, a motion for an investigation was defeated in Parliament.

o   In a 1989 report, the Istanbul Branch of the Human Rights Association described an incident that took place on September 12, 1989, in Siirt-Bangir. Soldiers came upon two shepherds taking their animals to water. The soldiers ordered the shepherds to lie on their

8

backs; soldiers then fatally shot one of them, named Zahit, through the head. The report details a number of other atrocities committed by security forces.

o   On May 23, 1990, the Turkish Human Rights Foundation announced that interrogation was underway in the "accidental shooting" of a villager named Besir Algan, who had not heeded a call to stop in the Budakli village of Mardin's Midyat township. Three SHP members of Parliament charged that Algan had been killed unjustly, and said they would raise the issue in Parliament.

Recent "Intifada" Tactics

Because winters in the southeast are extremely harsh, the fighting dies down for several months, and erupts again in the spring. In the spring of 1990 the fighting again intensified; during the first three weeks of May, 60 people died, of whom 37 were said to be PKK members. But this time new tactics were added: demonstrations, shop closings, and stone-throwing -- a strategy that has been labeled "The Kurdish Intifada."

According to reports in the Turkish press, Kamuran Dundar, the son of a member of the Nusaybin local council, was buried on March 15, 1990; he had been shot as a terrorist by security forces. Following the burial, Nusaybin residents confronted security forces, threw stones at them, and shouted slogans like, "Long live Kurdistan," and "Down with the Turkish State." Security forces fired on the crowds, killing one person, Semsettin Ciftci. Three hundred people were detained.

On March 19, Kurds demonstrated in Cizre to protest the security forces' actions in Nusaybin, closing their shops and staging a general strike. On March 20, security forces fired on crowds in Cizre who were trying to stage a demonstration; four people were killed and nine wounded. Sixty-eight people were detained.

On March 21, a university student in Diyarbakir, Zekiye Alkan, immolated herself in a protest against "the oppression of the Kurdish people." At the same time, thousands of Kurdish university students demonstrated to celebrate Newroz, the Kurdish New Year.

On March 26, shops and businesses in Cizre, Silopi and Idil remained closed, as residents launched a silent protest against "state terrorism." The next day, high school students in Cizre began a protest demonstration. When security forces ordered them to disperse, they refused, set fire to tires in the streets and threw stones at security forces. Rioting then followed in other sections of town. Four people were killed and nine seriously wounded by security forces. Police then detained 138 people, of whom 74 were formally arrested on March 28 by the State Security Court in Diyarbakir. On May 21, prosecutors asked for 10-year sentences for 155 Kurds accused of taking part in the demonstration; the defendants were charged with separatist propaganda, holding illegal rallies and damaging government property.

Following the incidents in Nusaybin and Cizre, shopkeepers in Diyarbakir, Silvan, Batman and Tunceli pulled down their shutters and closed their shops as a form of protest. The government reinforced its troops in the region and set up roadblocks at the entrances to towns, allowing entry only to government officials and local residents. Security forces intensified their military efforts; on April 7, 21 PKK combatants were killed and 15 captured.

During the first week in April, President Turgut Ozal met with the National Security Council and then announced that the events in the southeast "were part of a plan targeting the territorial integrity of the Turkish Republic." He called a "summit meeting" of the leaders of the three parties represented in Parliament to discuss additional measures to be targeted at the State of Emergency region.

Many observers in Turkey told us in early May that the events in the southeast had worried the government; that President Ozal had been forced to acknowledge that the unrest represented more than isolated terrorist incidents; and that recent events indicated a higher level of support for the PKK, or at least greater opposition to the government's policies in the region, than had been seen earlier.

We were told by many people in southeast Turkey that support for the PKK was mounting. One lawyer said support for the group varies from region to region; in some areas everyone supports the PKK -- in others 65 percent or less. But he believes that every year there is more and more sympathy for the militants because of the killings, detentions, beatings and harassment by security forces, which are bitterly resented by the Kurds in villages and in towns alike. In April, Reuters quoted Muslum Yildirim, the Mayor of Nusaybin, as saying that "about 95 percent" of the people in his town cooperated with the PKK "willingly." (On April 20, Yildirim was suspended from his position because of this statement.)

Decree 413

Following President Ozal's "summit meeting" with the leaders of the three parties in Parliament, Decree 413 was issued by the Council of Ministers on April 9, 1990. The decree equips Hayri Kozakcioglu, the regional governor of ten provinces under a state of emergency in southeastern Turkey, with extraordinary powers to censor the press, exile people who present a "danger to law and order," remove judges and public prosecutors, and suspend trade union rights. The decree provides that Kozakcioglu can:

o   censor the press by banning, confiscating, and heavily fining publications that "wrongly represent incidents occurring in a region which is under a state of emergency, disturbing its readers with distorted news stories or commentaries, causing anxiety among people in the region and obstructing security forces in the performance of their jobs;"

o   shut down printing plants that print such publications;

o   exile to other parts of Turkey people who "act against the state," the relocation sites to be chosen by the Ministry of the Interior;

o   control or prohibit all union activities, including strikes and lockouts; prevent boycotts, slow-downs, and the closing down of workplaces;

o   require State Security Court Public Prosecutors to open cases against people who violate Decree 413;

o   evacuate villages "for security reasons" without prior notice;

o   transfer "harmful" state employees.

Penalties for people convicted of supporting separatist activities were doubled. The decree also increased the penalties for publications that insult the president, Parliament, the government, state ministers, judges, and high-level state executives. The penal code provides for penalties of up to three years of imprisonment for such insults; the new decree adds fines of up to $40,000, of which the "responsible editor" (the person who, according to Turkish law, bears legal responsibility for the contents of the publication) must pay half.

In addition, Turkish Radio and Television broadcasts concerning the state of emergency region will be controlled by the Interior Ministry and the General Secretariat of the National Security Council.

Moreover, the powers of the regional governor extend even beyond the southeast; he has the authority to ban or confiscate an offending publication anywhere in Turkey. This means that he can censor the press in Istanbul or shut down a printing house in Ankara, for example. Even more disturbing is the fact that his actions may not be challenged in court; Article 148 of the Constitution forbids review by the Constitutional Court of decrees passed on the basis of state of emergency laws. The only entity required to approve the governor's actions is the Ministry of the Interior, which issues the final order. The governor's extensive powers were granted administratively by the Council of Ministers; Parliament had no say in the matter.

On May 9, the regional governor's powers were expanded even further: the Council of Ministers gave him the authority to deport from the area judges, prosecutors and military personnel. This means that the governor can remove from a case a prosecutor or judge who does not handle a matter to his satisfaction. This is indeed an extraordinary power.

Effects of Decree 413

The effects of Decree 413 were immediate and far-reaching. News of events in the Kurdish areas in southeastern Turkey was promptly censored -- directly by the regional governor, and indirectly by self-censorship on the part of the press. The language in the decree is both broad and vague; no guidelines have been issued to inform publishers what can and cannot be printed. In Istanbul, journalists for mainstream newspapers told the Helsinki mission that news items that had been routinely printed before the decree were either not printed now or were modified in hopes that the regional governor would not object. Articles in the press openly discussed self-censorship. Altan

14

Oyman wrote in *Milliyet* on April 17, 1990, that "publishing a report which is not openly 'confirmed' by the regional governor is a serious risk."

"This [decree] is heartbreaking, anti-democratic and difficult to oppose," the editor of a major national newspaper who preferred to remain anonymous told *The Los Angeles Times* (April 21, 1990). "They can catch you on anything. Suppose I send a reporter to the southeast and he is sentenced to 15 years, we are fined heavily and shut down. Is it worth it?"

Mehmet Ali Birand wrote in his column in *Milliyet* on April 17: "I wrote an article about the decree today, but the newspaper administration, thinking it was too risky to publish, told me to write another, 'just in case.'" He then apologized to his readers for not being able to write about certain subjects while the decree is in effect. (*Dateline*, April 21, 1990.)

As for the left-wing press, the effect was disastrous. Printing plants simply refused to print journals that they feared would cause the plants to be shut down. Mustafa Gursel reported in *The Turkish Daily News* on April 18 that "The owners of printing houses are in a panic; the police were going around Istanbul last week to printing houses and telling them they should not print certain publications." One printer, Hasan Basri Gurses, the owner of Bizim Offset, a printing house that printed left-wing journals and books, was arrested on April 30, 1990, and detained for three days. *Gunes* reported on June 19 that Cetin Tasci had been detained briefly for photocopying the periodical *Deng*. Mr. Tasci reported that he had been insulted and beaten while in detention.

2000'e Dogru (*Toward 2000*), the most influential of the left-wing magazines and one of the largest, missed two issues. In an interview with *Info-Turk*, Huseyin Karanlik, the journal's editor-in-chief, reported:

> After the decree was officially published, *Hurriyet* [printing house] authorities asked to meet with us. We discussed the risks of *Hurriyet*'s whole printing facility being closed down. On April 13, the contract was cancelled. We contacted several printing plants in an effort to get printed by someone else. Nafiz Ilicak agreed to print the magazine. But later they told us that authorities from the police department had warned them not to sign the contract.

Info-Turk reported in its April issue that President Ozal said on April 18, referring to *Hurriyet's* refusal to print *2000'e Dogru*, "The decree has already served its purpose." The magazine subsequently began being printed clandestinely.

For the small socialist journals that have been in continuous trouble with the government,[3] the decree was a calamity. At least eighteen journals were unable to find printers who were willing to risk printing their issues. Among these were: *Sokak (Street), Hedef (Target), Eylem (Action), Halk Gercegi (The People's Truth), Devrinci Genclik (Revolutionary Youth), Emek Dunyasi (The World of Work), Isciler ve Politika (Workers and Politics), Adimlar (Steps), Komun (Commune), Deng (Voice), Emegin Bayragi (Flag of the Workforce), Iscelerin Sesi (The Workers' Voice), Yeni Demokrasi (New Democracy), Toplumsal Kurtulus (Social Liberation), Yeni Cozum (New Solution), and Ozgurluk Dunyasi (Freedom of the World)*. A June issue of *Deng* was subsequently photocopied and distributed; authorities then confiscated it because it contained Kurdish language lessons.

On May 18, representatives of 17 periodicals met in Istanbul to discuss how to cope with the decree; police raided the meeting and detained all 17. All but three were released that afternoon. Mehmet Ali Eser of *Yeni Demokrasi*, Necdet Kanbir of *Toplumsal Kurtulus*, and a third journalist are still in detention.

In the southeast, censorship is more direct. A journalist in Diyarbakir told the Helsinki mission that the only news his newspaper was printing about events in the region was articles that were telefaxed to it by the Regional Governor's press office. When his newspaper writes a story on its own, it telefaxes it to the governor's press office before printing it. The press office generally returns the article, saying "this is not true." The newspaper then does not print it. "I can write about the PKK's actions, what they did," he said, "but I can't write about their reasons for taking the steps they did. For the time being we are not free; we are journalists of the government."

This journalist told us of two recent events that he had been unable to write about: one was the killing of three village guards in Hakkari -- the regional governor's office said it hadn't happened. In the other case, four village guards were in a car in Silopi district of

---

[3] See *Paying the Price: Freedom of Expression in Turkey*, Helsinki Watch, March 1989; and *News from Turkey: Freedom of Expression*, Helsinki Watch, February 1990.

16

Mardin during the last week of April. A bomb exploded in the car; three of them are still in the hospital in Diyarbakir. The regional governor's office denied that the incident had taken place.

"I am also forbidden to write the word 'Kurd,'" he told us. "That means that I am a person who has no identification; this makes me very unhappy."

Another journalist told us, "This is a difficult and terrifying kind of life, being careful every moment in order not to be put in prison."

The disturbing result of Decree 413 is therefore self-censorship on the part of the press, and, in some situations, prior censorship by officials. And the over-all effect is very dangerous: as one human rights activist in the southeast told us, "If the police do something wrong, no one will know about it, no one can look into it. It's very, very dangerous. We can't control what the police do, especially to people who are not educated, and have no idea about their rights. Because of this decree, the police are much freer to abuse people and to kill them. And people can't even go to court to try to get help."

A Diyarbakir resident told us, "On April 28th I saw out of my window five policemen beating two youths. They said, 'We can kill you, we can do whatever we want to you.' It was terrible -- there was nothing I could do."

Late in June, *Gunes* reported that the regional governor, Hayri Kozakcioglu, had begun to deport public employees in accordance with the power given to him by Decree 413. Sirlin Tetik, an employee of the Social Insurance System in Batman, was sent to Kirsehir; Mr. Tetik was a founder of the Diyarbakir branch of the Human Rights Association, and is presently on its board. Ramazan Tas, an employee of the PTT in Hakkari, was sent to Adapazari. Suleyman Kondakci of the Electricity Board was sent from Hakkari to Cankiri.

The Government's Defense of Decree 413

On April 15, President Ozal defended the issuance of Decree 413, saying in a televised speech that "these measures are aimed at the preservation of the integrity of the Turkish state with its nation and territory, within the framework of the powers and responsibilities defined in our Constitution." He denied that the powers to control the press amounted to censorship: "the measures envisage self-control by

17

the press in line with our national needs." He also denied that the authority to relocate people from the region amounted to sending people into exile.

Reaction to the Decree

Both Erdal Inonu, the leader of the main opposition party, the Social Democratic Populist Party (SHP), and Suleyman Demirel, the chairman of the True Path Party (DYP), called for a debate in Parliament on the measures contained in the decree. Nineteen independent deputies held a two-day vigil in Parliament urging a Parliamentary debate. Speaker of Parliament Kaya Erdem, of Ozal's Motherland Party (ANAP), has also urged such a debate. Human rights activists, lawyers and journalists sharply criticized the human rights violations effected by the decree. Some called the decree "martial law in disguise." *Hurriyet* called the decree "reminiscent of one of the most repressive laws in the history of the Turkish Republic: Takrir-i Sukun, a law for the establishment of public order issued in 1925 after the Sheik Sait Uprising in Turkish Kurdistan." As of this writing, the decree is in effect and has not been debated in Parliament.

Meanwhile, public protests against the decree have been mounting in the southeast; the Turkish Human Rights Foundation reported on May 30, 1990, that 1,058 detainees and convicted prisoners had gone on hunger strikes to protest the decree, and that 566 people had carried out hunger strikes at the Diyarbakir headquarters of the Socialist Party in support of the prisoners. On June 22, a petition protesting Decree 413 was presented to the Foreign Ministry; it contained 15,000 signatures that had been collected by writers for socialist magazines.

Village Guards

In order to protect villages in the southeast from guerrilla actions, the Turkish government has set up a system of village guards -- local peasants who are given arms and paid monthly salaries. The guards act as a paramilitary force, supplementing the police, the army and the gendarmerie.[4] Regional Governor Kozakcioglu announced on June 15, 1990, that there were 21,480 village guards. Village guards are specifically targeted by the PKK; the Turkish press regularly reports on clashes in which village guards have been killed. In recent months, thousands of villagers have abandoned their villages, leaving their homes, schools, fields and fruit trees, rather than provide village guards for the military.

The Turkish government contends that village guards are volunteers. On May 31, 1988, for example, then-Minister of the Interior Mustafa Kalemli said: "We are not forcing anyone to register as a village guard. We have only volunteers, patriots who are against the separatists."

In May 1990, the Helsinki mission found evidence that casts doubt on the government's assertions. According to leaders in Siirt, a town about 140 miles east of Diyarbakir, at least 950 people had come to Siirt during the last ten days of April 1990, abandoning their villages. In Siirt we interviewed men from three villages that have been abandoned by all of their inhabitants, who have left their homes rather than provide village guards for the security forces, and from a fourth village which has been half-emptied for the same reason.

o   Azad K.,[5] a 35-year-old villager with a wife and seven children, ages one to 15, from the village of Kelleh in Sivikice, about a three-hour drive from the town of Siirt, reported that soldiers had come to Kelleh in April 1990 and told the village mukhtar (headman) that the

---

[4] For a fuller discussion of the village guard system, see *State of Flux: Human Rights in Turkey*, Helsinki Watch, December 1987.

[5] The names of witnesses interviewed by the Helsinki mission, and of the villagers whom they identified, have been changed for their protection.

village had to provide 15 village guards. Mr. K. said that the villagers did not want to be village guards, as they didn't want to be enemies of the PKK and of other villages. Village guards are sometimes made to fight against other villages in the area. The village of Kelleh refused to provide 15 guards. On April 17, 1990, between 16 and 20 soldiers returned to Kelleh and told the people they had to leave the village because they supported the PKK. The soldiers insisted that the villagers had given food to the PKK; Mr. K. said they had not.

The villagers were told they had to leave in two days, but one day later, the soldiers came again, attacked the villagers and told them to leave immediately. Mr. K. was beaten by Sergeant Kemal, who used his fists and boots, but no weapons. One villager lost his teeth in a beating. Sergeant Kemal said, " Leave the village or I'll burn it." The villagers left.

Some villagers returned later to see what the army had done, and found that they had killed all the animals -- hens and turkeys -- had collected the eggs, taken food, broken doors and windows of houses and smashed furniture. They had not burned the wheat.

The villagers took with them what they could, and have sold their possessions to survive. Some are living in tents in Siirt, some have gone to other parts of the southeast. Mr. K. and his family are living in a nearby village with relatives.

o   Welat M., a 32-year-old man with a wife and five children, ages one to six, had lived in the village of Besah, in Siirt Province. Soldiers came to Besah on April 17, 1990, and told the inhabitants that they would have to provide village guards, and that if they didn't, they would have to leave the village. The soldiers accused the villagers of supporting the PKK. Mr. M. told the Helsinki mission that when the PKK had come to the village, they were given bread; that the villagers did not agree with the PKK, but were afraid not to give them bread.

The soldiers told the villagers they had to leave within 24 hours. The next day the soldiers returned and beat the villagers, including women and children. "You can't imagine how many times I was beaten in the same day. One of the old men, Haci L., was beaten unconscious. Another old man, Azad D., had half his beard torn off, and was also beaten unconscious." Inhabitants were hit with sticks, rifle butts and fists and were kicked. Soldiers shot at one 35-year-old man, who threw himself into his house to avoid being killed. The villagers did not try to fight the soldiers, but kept asking them, "Why are you doing this? Why do you behave like this?"

This was not the first time the army had told villagers they had to be village guards, and the army had attacked the village many times. Some of the villagers had left earlier, but now all have left. They had to leave their houses, their equipment, their tools, their wheat, their fruit trees. The soldiers took their horses, their furniture and everything people had owned, including gold and jewelry meant for dowries for their daughters.

Mr. M. and his family are now living in a tent in Siirt; he brought the tent from his village. Winters are very harsh, and the tent doesn't protect them from the cold.

"Life is very dangerous," Mr. M. said. "It's too dangerous for us to go back to our village. The soldiers told us they would bomb our village and say the PKK did it."

o   Mustafa D., a 30-year-old man with a wife and four children, from 4 to 6, had lived in the village of Cema, in Perani. All the villagers left Cema in October 1989.

21

The previous month, soldiers had asked villagers to accept weapons and act as village guards. The men refused. As a result, they had been attacked by the army many times. They were told they had to become village guards or leave their village.

At one point, all the men of the village were taken to the gendarme station and beaten with sticks, stones and rifle butts, and kicked. Mr. D. was beaten unconscious three times. Families were beaten in the village as well; children were beaten too. On one occasion, four soldiers beat him and his children.

Mr. D. and his family are now living in the town of Siirt in tents, along with 14 other families from Cema. Last winter two of his children, boys 3 and 7, died from illnesses contracted during the harsh winter. When they left the village, they could take nothing but their tents. They have no fuel to keep them warm. Mr. D. works in the fields of other villages when he can; he earns a daily rate of TL 3,000 (about $1.20).

"We want to go back to our village, and resume our life there. We want the government not to touch us. We are hungry here. We don't want to be tortured by the state and the soldiers. I had bought some wheat and a tractor, and had paid for it all," Mr. D. said. "I had to leave it all behind, and the soldiers told village guards from other villages to take it."

o   Haci B., a 28-year-old man with a wife and one child, lives in the village of Erkent, in Pervari district. One year ago there were 120 families living there; now there are only 70. The rest of the families left because the army wanted them to provide village guards. Most have gone to Cikurova or Adana. Mr. B. said he has to stay to take care of his land, which is very good. The army won't let him or the other shepherds take their animals out to pasture where they used to go; now they have to graze the animals very close to the village.

22

As a result, there is not enough food for the animals, and many are dying. In the last two years, the village has lost at least 3,000 animals, mostly sheep; they used to have 10,000. The soldiers won't permit the shepherds to take their sheep to the valley, on the grounds that they would give their sheep and bread to the PKK there. Also, the villagers are not permitted to visit their friends in other villages.

Several months ago, ten men were taken from Mr. B.'s village to army headquarters in Diyarbakir and accused of supporting the PKK, although Mr. B. said they were not. They were tortured for 20 days at the police station in Siirt and then taken to prison, where they served three months. They were freed during the first week in April.

Two other men from Erkent, Bedri E. and Azad G., visited Kopricoy village in January 1990. Police made them take off their clothes, pushed them into mud, and then displayed them to all the villagers, naked and covered with mud.

The Helsinki mission visited the village of Beluris, half an hour's drive outside of the town of Siirt. The village contains 65 houses in which 500 people used to live. As a result of harassment by the military, the village had been abandoned. Two months before our visit, two of the original families had returned to the village, along with four families from other villages. One of the villagers, Ali Y. (not his real name), told us that the village had been attacked by the military in February 1988. The men in the village were beaten and thrown into the mud. The army told them they had to fight the PKK or leave the village. Gradually all of the families left. Mr. Y. had returned to take care of his land and to graze his animals.

During the drive to Beluris, we were shown from a distance three other villages that had been abandoned by their inhabitants because of pressure from the military.

Amnesty International has reported on the mistreatment of villagers who have refused to become village guards. In an Urgent Action communique dated 25 January 1990, Amnesty said:

In mid-1989 many villagers in Cukurca district refused to continue working as village protectors, who are paid by the government to fight Kurdish guerrillas operating in the area, and gave their arms back to the authorities. According to a press report inhabitants of Uzumdere, Cigli, Koprulu and Uzumlu villages were asked by the authorities to take up arms again. Those who refused were reportedly subjected to torture and ill-treatment and some 250 people were detained in December. Most were released after a short while, but 42 were taken to Diyarbakir State Security Court on 22 December. Six inhabitants of Uzumlu village were formally arrested on charges of having supported the Kurdish guerrillas. Relatives who visited them in prison reportedly saw wounds on their hands and the soles of their feet alleged to be the result of torture.

Hurriyet reported on October 23, 1989:

A Kurdish peasant, Ismail Keskin, was tortured at the Army Headquarters in Hakkari for not having agreed to become a village guard. After torture, Keskin's wounds were treated at the State Hospital in Hakkari.

Middle East International reported on February 2, 1990, that hundreds of families in Van province had been forced to leave their villages:

Local observers say some 7,000 Kurds from more than 200 villages have left for the towns in the last four months. In Van alone there are more than 3,000 migrants.

Kaya Oner, leader of the Sidan tribe of 14,000 villagers southeast of Van, says he has already been punished for his refusal to cooperate. In September last year, at a meeting between the province's aghas and the authorities, he refused to order his people to take up government weapons. Five days later, he says, the military drove up to his brother's house and shot him dead before the whole village. "The government wanted to show me that even the aghas are not safe. It refuses to allow people who do not want to be involved to get on with

24

their lives. It wants to draw a clear line between the two sides; if you are not on the authorities' side, then they consider you PKK and treat you like PKK."

Yavuz Binbay of the Van Human Rights Organization claims that the military is pursuing a systematic policy of intimidation in the region's villages in order to chase out those who refuse to fight the guerrillas.

In the village of Dalbasi, south of Van, 40 of the 60 houses stand empty. Since the PKK entered the village, kidnapped three young men and burned down the school, the teacher, the mukhtar (local official) and those with enough money have moved away. On what remains of the burned out school, the military have scrawled their war on the guerrillas in words: "The star of the morning (the PKK emblem) has no chance -- come be a man and fight with us."

In a report issued in late 1989, the Diyarbakir branch of the Human Rights Association said:

As a consequence of the continuing oppression and terrorist tactics, nearly all of the villages in the area surrounding Mt.Cudi and 374 of the villages between Catak (near Van) and the region's border with Siirt have been emptied. In the past three months about 30,000 people have immigrated into the provincial capital of Van from the rural areas and some of the county towns.

The policy of the village militia system and the policy of forced armament of the population have thrown the society into a state of chaos. In order to guarantee that the damage imposed on the society can be repaired, and that no further irreparable damage is done, the village militia system must be brought to an end and the process of armament must be stopped immediately.

In an alarming new development, the weekly *Tempo* reported on May 27, 1990, that Mahmut Alinak, a member of Parliament from Kars, had said in a speech in Parliament that "mines were laid around

25

villages in Cukurca township in the southeastern province of Hakkari that had rejected the scheme of village guards." He also stated that Hikmet Demir, from Kurudere village, had died and seven others had been injured when one of those mines was detonated. Arif Keskin and Eyup Korkmaz also lost their lives in mine explosions in Cayirli Village. Alinak's speech was not reported in any newspaper because of the restrictions contained in Decree 413.

Sometimes villages are evacuated because of their proximity to borders through which the government believes PKK guerrillas come into Turkey. According to *Hurriyet* (January 29, 1990), for example:

> The evacuation of villages and settlements within 600 meters of Turkey's border with Iraq has begun. The people of the region have expressed their opposition to the move and claimed that they realized they were being forced to move after military units had them sign blank forms.

> Meanwhile, a group of journalists from the *Hurriyet* news service who traveled on foot through snow to the village of Cayirli, 30 kilometers from Cukurca, to photograph the evacuated villages, were detained for 72 hours by Major Mustafa Nacak, commander of the gendarmerie battalion of the Cukurca border region.

And now Decree 413 provides that villages may be evacuated for "security reasons" without prior notice. *Gunes* reported on June 25 that some villages and hamlets on the Turkish-Iranian border were being vacated on the grounds that they "lacked security" and "provided shelter for PKK militants." The villagers were being settled in Hakkari city center, and in the townships of Yuksekova, Semdinli and Cukurca townships. The weekly *Tempo* said the villages were being vacated under the supervision of border commando units. Hakkari Member of Parliament Cumhur Keskin charged that the relocations were carried out for assimilation purposes in violation of the Constitution.

Arrests, Torture and Death

The Turkish government's pattern of detention, torture and formal arrest[6] is even more pronounced in southeastern Turkey than in the rest of the country. The Istanbul HRA branch reported in late 1989:

> During our investigations [in 10 towns in the southeast] we observed that in these regions, in which Kurds form the majority of the population, mass arrests and torture are being carried out with an even more alarming frequency than in the rest of Turkey.
>
> We found out that the family of a person under arrest is not notified in any way, and that he is prohibited from communicating in any way with the outside.
>
> As we stepped out of the City Hall of Mardin, we met relatives of persons under arrest. They told us that twelve people had been under arrest for the past 29 days, and that they were concerned about their condition. The relatives of those under arrest told us the names of three of these people: Cetin Azma from Yenikoy, and Salih Bolu and Mehmet Bedik from Silopi.
>
> On September 8, 1989, a placard with explosives attached to it was put up in the village of Derik in Mardin province... As a result of this incident, 15 people were arrested and subjected to torture. Only three of these people were brought to trial, and they were judged not guilty. The people who were arrested were asked while they were being tortured, "We know that you didn't do it. Name the people who could have done it. Who was spreading propaganda in the coffeehouses? . . ."
>
> Another villager from Derik, who does not want his identity known, told us that he is being put under constant pressure by the security forces, and that he has been arrested twice on the charge that he had given shelter to the PKK. During these

---

[6] See *News from Turkey: Eight Cases of Torture*, Helsinki Watch, July 1989.

arrests he was subjected to every kind of torture (high-pressure streams of cold water, electric shocks, etc.). He feared that if his name were published he would no longer be able to stay in the region.

In another incident that we were told about, the guests of a person named Tevfik Gorendogan in Catak were arrested and tortured on the charge that they were wearing a certain kind of boot. A craftsman who was selling boots of this type was arrested, because the shoes are part of the PKK uniform.

Since in most cases people are tortured during their detention with the knowledge of the public prosecutors and doctors, and because the special interrogation teams use their own doctors, it is not possible to prove that torture has taken place.

The Diyarbakir HRA reports cases of death from torture:

o   Dervis Savgat, of the village of Yukari Kosanlar, was taken from his house on August 25, 1988, by a political team which arrived in an automobile with official license plates. He was taken to the headquarters of the Political Division of Mardin, where he died. A dispute over the cause of his death was resolved by a commission of the public prosecutor of Viransehir that revealed that the neck, arms and legs of the corpse had been broken, the skull crushed, the testes were swollen, and the tip of the penis had turned black. The commission concluded that the death was the result of torture.

o   Osman Esendemir of Siirt was arrested on May 24, 1989, on orders of Major Ahmet Oktay, the battalion commander of the local gendarmerie. From then on he was used as a military courier. On June 3, 1989, Osman Esendemir was given an envelope by the major which he was supposed to take to the gendarmerie in Ormanici village. The major said, "Your work for me is now ended." Osman Endemir told his family about this conversation, and took with him his relatives

Nimet and Omer Esendemir and set out. Shortly
thereafter, six people came toward them on the
Derbest Square. Three of them -- militiamen Aktug,
Ramazan and Abdulkerim Bahattin -- came over to
them and sent Nimet and Omer home, saying, "Osman
came on account of us. We have to take care of
something with Osman. You go home." Osman
Esendemir disappeared on that day. His family then
searched the square and found his corpse; it had been
cut into pieces. Lawyer Zubeyir Aydar pressed charges
at the office of the public prosecutor, but no conclusion
has been reached.

Abuse of Civilians

The Turkish government continues to abuse civilians in the southeast. Authorities are still investigating an incident that took place in Yesilyurt village in Mardin province on the night of January 14, 1989, two days after two police officers were killed by PKK militants in the area. According to village officials, gendarmes gathered all male village inhabitants in the town square and asked for information about the police deaths. When they received no information, they forced the men to lie on the ground, beat them and forced them to eat human excrement. An army major, Cafer Tayyar Caglayan, was charged with responsibility for these acts and tried in May 1990. On June 13, 1990, he was convicted and sentenced to a prison sentence of two months and 15 days. His sentence, however, was then converted to a fine and deferred. The court reported that no evidence substantiated villagers' claims that they had been forced to eat excrement, but that evidence showed that soldiers had beaten villagers on Caglayan's orders.

Early in September 1989, provincial governors banished as "undesirable elements" eight men from Siirt and one from Tunceli. No court hearing was held, and the governors had no apparent authority for the action. The eight from Siirt were all members of the SHP (the Social Democratic Populist Party), the main opposition party. One, Zubeyir Aydar, a former SHP province chairman, is a lawyer who had been investigating a case in which dozens of corpses had been found early in the year buried at "Butcher's River" in Siirt, some reportedly victims of torture.

The Helsinki mission interviewed Mr. Aydar in Siirt in May. Mr. Aydar, who is the chairman of the Siirt branch of the Turkish Human Rights Association, had been ordered to leave Siirt within 24 hours. He told us that his exile had lasted for three months. Since his return, many people have reported to him that the security forces have told them not to talk with Mr. Aydar, or to give him any legal business. In addition, he has received death threats because of legal steps he took recently. His legal actions took place following a demonstration in the nearby town of Batman on April 3, 1990, in which shopkeepers closed their shops to protest the government's actions in Cizre, described earlier in this report. Siirt Governor Atilla Koc, Siirt Police Chief Ismail Bardakci, and Batman Mayor Ali Ulger went to the Oncu Pharmacy. Governor Koc ordered the owner to open his shop. When the owner refused, Koc told Mayor Ulger to break the shop windows. Ulger did so; when the Oncu's owner tried to stop him, Ulger hit the owner. Then police officers acting on Bardakci's orders went through the town breaking shop windows and doors with big hammers; they also stole property from the shops. Aydar said total losses exceeded TL 100 million (about $40,000). Townspeople in Batman called Aydar to report; on arriving in Batman, Aydar saw broken windows and doors everywhere -- "it looked like a war scene," he said.

The next day, April 4, Aydar filed an application in court, asking the Public Prosecutor to open a case against the three officials for their actions. No case has yet been opened. Ten days later, Aydar was told by two people that Governor Koc had threatened to kill him.

Doctors, too, are at risk. A doctor in Diyarbakir told the Helsinki mission about another doctor, Dr. Abdullah Bolca, the director of Cizre Hospital in Mardin, who had treated a patient whom the police believed to be a PKK member. Police detained Dr. Bolca in September 1989, tortured him for 15 days and then released him. Dr. Bolca was then dismissed from his position and sent from Cizre to Yozgat in Western Turkey. *Info-Turk* reported in October 1989 that Dr. Bolca said on his release: "I have no relations with the PKK. My duty as a doctor is to give medical care to whoever is in need. I cannot know if the patient is a terrorist or not. Furthermore, I am not obliged to verify it; it is not my duty."

In a recent incident that is indicative of the strong feelings and taboos associated with the Turkish Kurds, seven Kurdish members of Parliament belonging to the SHP politcal party were expelled from the party in November 1989 because they had taken part in a high-level conference on the Kurds in Paris the preceding month. The seven deputies are Mehmet Ali Eren, Kenan Sonmez and Ismail Hakki Onal from Istanbul, Ahmet Turk and Adnan Ekmen from Mardin, Salik Sumer from Diyarbakir, and Mahmut Alinak from Kars.

A similar incident took place in January 1989, when SHP Member of Parliament Ibrahim Aksoy made a speech at a Turkey-European Joint Parliamentary Commission meeting in Strasbourg saying that Kurds exist and should be treated as a people. He called for an end to discrimination against Kurds. As a result, he was branded a separatist by the SHP and in February 1989 was expelled from the SHP for two years.

The Turkish press reported on May 10, 1990, that the Parliament's Judicial Commission had recommended lifting the

Parliamentary immunity of three independent deputies -- Ibrahim Aksoy, Mehmet Ali Eren and Tevfik Kocak, as well as SHP deputy Fikri Saglar -- to allow them to be charged legally for their "statements and activities regarding the Kurdish problem." According to a Turkish Human Rights Foundation report, President Ozal had earlier proposed such action against deputies who attract attention by their activities related to the "Kurdish problem."

Actions on the Kurdish issue have reached ridiculous heights; for example, on January 10, 1990, a German sociologist, Hella Schlumberger, was detained in Siirt because of an entry in a visitors' book at Birecik Bald Ibis Breeding Station that was deemed separatist propaganda. Ms. Schlumberger had written, "Long live the soil of Kurdistan, long live freedom." She was acquitted and released on January 23rd, after strong pressure from the West German government. Amnesty International reported on January 31 that two brothers, Irfan and Mahmut Sahin, were detained for two days because they had invited Ms. Schlumberger to visit their home after her release.

Due Process in Legal Proceedings

On September 26, 1989, then-Prime Minister Turgut Ozal signed a decree that provided that detainees in police custody be given immediate access to attorneys. Yucel Onen, the president of the Diyarbakir Bar Association, told the Helsinki mission in May that for a short period it had been possible for lawyers in Diyarbakir to meet with their clients shortly after detention, but that it soon became impossible again.[7]

Mr. Onen reported on a number of other problems encountered by lawyers in Diyarbakir: first, although families are now permitted to talk in Kurdish with prisoners, lawyers are still forbidden to do do so. This means that in those cases in which prisoners do not speak Turkish, lawyers cannot adequately prepare a defense. In

---

[7] Turgut Kazan, the president of the Istanbul Bar Association, told the Helsinki mission in Istanbul in May 1990 that Ozal's decree had never been enforced, with the exception of a handful of cases. As an example, he provided the mission with a copy of a form letter dated February 12, 1990, denying lawyer Husnu Ondal the right to meet with Muzaffer Ilhan Erdost, a publisher detained on charges of "separatist propaganda." The letter stated that the lawyer could not see Erdost during the investigation of his case because it would "hinder the investigation." Erdost was released the following day.

Mr. Kazan reported that the decree contains many loopholes: the defendant must ask for a lawyer to whom he has previously given the right to represent him, and the public prosecutor has to approve. No method of appeal is provided, if the request is denied. If the detainee has not previously asked a lawyer to represent him, and requests to see a notary public to make such a request, police deny the request. Mr. Kazan believes that the decree was issued to give the west the image that defendants' rights are safeguarded in Turkey.

The Istanbul Bar Association has urged that detainees have immediate, private access to an attorney; that attorneys must be present during interrogation; and that a detainee must be allowed to ask the help of one or more attorneys at any time, including during the preliminary investigation.

For an exhaustive study of the Turkish legal system's response to torture, see *Torture in Turkey: the Legal System's Response*, Committee on International Human Rights of the Association of the Bar of the City of New York, 1989.

addition, lawyers are not given enough time to prepare their cases, cannot talk privately with prisoners, cannot get from officials all the necessary documents relating to the charges, and are never permitted to talk with detainees in police stations. There has been one improvement in the last few years: it is now possible to see prisoners for an hour or more to prepare a case (a few years ago, lawyers were allowed only five minutes to meet with prisoners).

Mr. Onen said that the authorities attempt to frighten lawyers; if lawyers use strong language in defending a client, or criticize government policy toward the Kurds in court, the lawyers themselves may be prosecuted. Such prosecutions took place with some frequency in the past, but none has occurred in the past 18 months. "There are many written documents, like the Universal Declaration of Human Rights, that protect people," said Mr. Onen, "but they are only on paper, and do not exist here in practice. It is sorrowful to see the state claiming to be a state of justice, when it is actually turning into a police state."

Denial of Ethnic Identity

Examples of the government's denial of the Kurds' ethnic identity are not hard to come by. In May 1989, the National Security Council launched a campaign denying the existence of a distinct Kurdish nation and a Kurdish language. Pamphlets were issued and distributed to schools in the southeast, claiming that Kurdish is not a distinct language, but a dialect of Turkish. Kurdish prisoners who attempt to defend themselves in court in Kurdish are removed from court, and thus cannot conduct their defense. Mehdi Zana, the former mayor of Diyarbakir, who has been in prison since 1980 charged with separatist activities, now faces another 15-year sentence for using Kurdish in his defense statement.

Although before the issuance of Decree 413, the mainstream press was freer to use the word "Kurd" and to write about Turkish Kurds in the southeast, many left-wing journals that reported regularly on the Kurds were confiscated and their editors charged with various offenses and sometimes detained and tortured by police. In at least ten cases since March 1989, *2000'e Dogru (Toward 2000)* has been charged with "making propaganda to weaken nationalist feelings," or "Kurdish propaganda" for articles on Turkish Kurds; at least four issues were confiscated from newsstands for such articles.

Ismail Besikci, a Turkish sociologist who has served 10 years in prison for his writings on the Kurds, was arrested in March for his book entitled, *Kurdistan: A Colony of Many Nations,* and charged with separatist propaganda. Besikci's trial began in May, and the court refused to release him from prison. Meanwhile, two other books of his were confiscated: *Science/Official Ideology, State Democracy and The Kurdish Question,* and *An Intellectual, An Organization and the Kurdish Problem.* Besikci faces possible sentences of forty-five years in prison for the three books. Helsinki Watch has strongly protested his arrest. On June 20, police used truncheons to disperse a crowd of 300 people who were protesting authorities' refusal to permit them to attend Besikci's trial. Twenty protesters were detained; on June 21, 13 of them were arrested and sent to Bayrampasa prison, charged with holding an illegal demonstration. A petition containing 10,000 signatures was given to the Justice Ministry, asking for Besikci's release. Finally, on July 25, 1990, Ismail Besikci was released from prison; the three cases against him, however, are continuing.

Helsinki Watch regularly receives examples of the denial of Kurdish ethnic identity:

o   *Cumhuriyet* reported that 61-year-old Saliha Sener was sentenced to a one-year prison term in Diyarbakir on November 21, 1989, for speaking Kurdish during an election rally in March. The sentence was later converted to a fine of $1,150, which was eventually suspended provisionally -- to be reinstated if Ms. Sener broke the law again. In her testimony, given in Kurdish and translated into Turkish, Ms. Sener said: "I don't know Turkish. That's why I spoke in Kurdish." Later, Ms. Sener told the press: "I have never been educated and my family married me off at the age of 15. I am a villager. I have to speak Kurdish and accept the sentence. Even if they hang me I have to speak Kurdish because I am a Kurd."

o   In February 1990, an appeals court ruled that a Kurdish couple could not be prosecuted for giving their child a Kurdish name. "The choice of a name is a right exclusively personal; nobody can annul this right and leave a person nameless," said the court. Inquiries by the Helsinki mission in Diyarbakir in May, however, revealed that the decision is not being observed in practice; a Kurd who registers a child with a Kurdish name is still told that the name must be changed.

o   According to *Gunes* (March 10, 1990), Imam Abdullah Dinizhan was given a three-year prison sentence for giving a religious speech in Kurdish in a mosque.

o   The Turkish press reported on May 9, 1990, that a singer, Bedri Ayseli, who sang for SHP head Erdal Inonu at a dinner party in Diyarbakir, had been taken into custody because the song was in Kurdish. Officials of the hotel where the dinner took place were also taken to the Political Section of the Security Department. All were interrogated and released.

o   On June 26, *Tercuman* reported that the Ankara State
        Security Court has begun an investigation against
        members of Parliament Fuat Atalay and Cumhur
        Keskin for asking that the Turkish Radio and
        Television Company broadcast some programs in
        Kurdish. The grounds are "making separatist
        propaganda."

One Turkish intellectual told us, "The situation is the southeast
is getting worse all the time; our only hope is to grant the Kurds
cultural autonomy."

Violations of International Legal Standards

Both the PKK and the government of Turkey have violated international legal standards by their policies and actions in southeast Turkey.

Internal armed conflicts are covered by Common Article 3 of the 1949 Geneva Conventions, to which Turkey is a party. That article provides that:

> In the case of armed conflict not of an international character occurring in the territory of one of the High Contracting Parties, each Party to the conflict shall be bound to apply, as a minimum, the following provisions:
>
> (1) Persons taking no active part in the hostilities, including members of armed forces who have laid down their arms . . . shall in all circumstances be treated humanely...
>
> To this end, the following acts are and shall remain prohibited at any time and in any place whatsoever with respect to the above-mentioned persons:
>
> (a)   violence to life and person, in particular murder of all kinds, mutilation, cruel treatment and torture;
>
> (b)   taking of hostages;
>
> (c)   outrages upon personal dignity, in particular humiliating and degrading treatment;
>
> (d)   the passing of sentences and the carrying out of executions without previous judgment pronounced by a regularly constituted court, affording all the judicial guarantees which are recognized by civilized peoples.

Both the Turkish government and the PKK have violated common Article 3 by the killing of innocent civilians, as documented earlier in this report. Security forces have also tortured and, on at least one occasion (the case of Osman Esendemir, above), mutilated a body.[8] Some of the killings by security forces appear to be summary executions in violation of (1)(d), for example the cases of Dervis Sagat and the shepherd, Zahit, reported earlier.

Section (1)(d) has also been violated by Turkey; that section requires sentences based on judgments pronounced by regularly constituted courts that afford "all the judicial guarantees which are recognized by civilized peoples." Lawyers' inability to speak with prisoners in Kurdish, to meet in privacy, and to secure all documents necessary for a person's defense, do not meet such guarantees.

Security forces have carried out humiliating and degrading treatment, forbidden by Section (1)(c), by forcing villagers to eat excrement; by stripping villagers, throwing them into the mud and exposing them to others; and by other actions documented in this report in the section on Abuse of the Civilian Population.

Forcible displacement of civilians in internal armed conflicts is covered by Article 17 of Protocol II to the 1949 Geneva Conventions:

> The displacement of the civilian population shall not be ordered for reasons related to the conflict unless the security of the civilians involved or imperative military reasons so demand. Should such displacements have to be carried out, all possible measures shall be taken in order that the civilian population may be received under satisfactory conditions of shelter, hygiene, health, safety and nutrition.

Although Turkey has not signed Protocol II, Helsinki Watch calls on the government of Turkey to adhere to this standard. The present choice given to villagers -- "provide village guards to assist the military, or leave your village" -- constitutes forcible displacement and punishment without due process of law, as do those cases in which the military simply orders villagers to leave. According to Protocol II, such displacements can be ordered in only two situations: for the security of the civilians involved, or for imperative military reasons. It is not clear that either of these conditions exists throughout southeastern Turkey;

---

[8] Desecration of corpses is forbidden by Article 8, Protocol II to the 1949 Geneva Conventions.

42

assuming for the sake of argument that they do, and that the government is justified in displacing some villages, the government has clearly failed in its concomitant obligation to provide to the displaced villagers "satisfactory conditions of shelter, hygiene, health, safety and nutrition."

One explanation for the security forces' displacement of villagers is the government's wish to deny the PKK a social base. Such an objective has nothing to do with the security of civilians. Nor can it be justified by "imperative military reasons" without "the most meticulous assessment of the circumstances,"[9] because such actions are so susceptible to abuse. Relocation of civilians to deny the PKK a social base is an attempt to control people who are seen as dissidents, and is a political, and not a military move. The criminal code can be used to prosecute people who provide material support to the guerrillas; but displacing civilians from their homes, their lands and their livelihood is a drastic step and cannot be undertaken lightly.

The forced conscription of villagers to act as paramilitary village guards apparently has no basis in Turkish law. Men of military age serve in the armed forces; if more soldiers are needed to combat guerrilla warfare in the southeast, the government could increase the size of the army and of the gendarmerie. Forcing shepherds to be village guards who carry weapons and are therefore legitimate targets of the PKK can, and often does, result in loss of life. This is certainly not the humane treatment required for non-combatants by Common Article 3 of the Geneva Conventions. In addition, the International Covenant on Civil and Political Rights, Article 4(2), expressly prohibits derogation from certain obligations, even during an emergency that threatens the life of the state. These non-derogable rights are the right to life, the prohibition against torture, cruel or degrading treatment, and the prohibition of slavery. Although Turkey has not signed the International Covenant on Civil and Political Rights, Helsinki Watch calls on the government of Turkey to adhere to its standards.

---

[9] International Committee of the Red Cross, *Commentary on the Additional Protocols of 1977 to the Geneva Conventions of 1949* at 1472.

Burning of schools by the PKK, as well as looting of abandoned villages by security forces, are forbidden by international customary law. Pillage is specifically outlawed by Article 4(2)(g) of Protocol II.

Recent information, noted earlier, indicates that the security forces have begun to use land mines in the southeast. The main source of international law concerning land mines is the Land Mines Protocol, annexed to the 1981 United Nations Conference on Prohibition or Restrictions on the Use of Certain Conventional Weapons Which May be Deemed to be Excessively Injurious and to have Indiscriminate Effects. It applies only to international armed conflicts and to a limited class of wars of national liberation. Helsinki Watch calls on the Turkish government to adhere to the standards it sets.

The Land Mines Protocol seeks to protect civilians from superfluous injury or unnecessary suffering; it is based on a customary principle of the laws of war -- namely, that the rights of the parties of an armed conflict to adopt methods or means of warfare are not unlimited.[10] Article 4(2) of the Land Mines Protocol forbids the use of hand-delivered mines or explosives in:

> any city, town, village or other area containing a similar concentration of civilians in which combat between ground forces is not taking place or does not appear to be imminent, unless either:
>
> (a) they are placed on or in the close vicinity of a military objective belonging to or under the control of an adverse party, or
>
> (b) measures are taken to protect civilians from their effects, for example, the posting of warning signs, the posting of sentries, the issue of warnings or the provision of fences.

---

[10] See United Nations Resolution 2444, which recognizes principles of customary international law.

As discussed earlier, Deputy Mahmut Alinak reported to Parliament in late May that mines had been laid around villages in Cukurca township that had rejected the village guard system. If this is true, the government is using the land mines to punish villagers who do not cooperate with it, and not against specific military objectives, and thus is in violation of the Land Mines Protocol. Because deaths of noncombatants have occurred through the use of mines in a manner that does not protect noncombatants, it is of course also in violation of Common Article 3 of the Geneva Conventions. Helsinki Watch calls on the government of Turkey to refrain from using land mines except in situations in which such use is clearly justified by international law.

Conditions in Refugee Camps for Iraqi Kurds

In Diyarbakir, the Helsinki mission met with Akram Mayi, an agricultural engineer who is a spokesperson for the Iraqi Kurds confined in a refugee camp 10 kilometers outside the center of Diyarbakir. Mr. Mayi told us that 29,800 of the original 100,000 Iraqi Kurds who fled Iraq twenty months ago are still in Turkey. He reported that 11,200 people are living in very crowded conditions in 71 apartment buildings in the camp in Diyarbakir. Food is barely adequate, and water is covered with an oily film and is piped in only at night. Seven thousand of the refugees are under 14; there are no schools and no play yards. The refugees tried to set up schools themselves (many are teachers), but police prohibited them, and would not set up schools to teach the children in Turkish, either. People are sometimes free to leave the camp; police can grant permission or not. Some refugees have been able to get work in Diyarbakir; their pay is low -- TL 5,000 to 10,000, the price of one kilogram of meat. With their earnings, they buy clothes for their children, or vegetables and fruit.

Mr. Mayi reported that 11,800 refugees live in inadequate tents in a camp in Kiziltepe, in Mardin Province. Their conditions are worse than those in Diyarbakir. Each person is allowed to leave the camp once a month, so securing work is impossible. Police beat the refugees for no reason; many have been wounded. The Turkish government had announced that it would build permanent housing in Yozgat, in Western Turkey, for the Kurds in Kiziltepe, but recently those plans were cancelled, so the Kiziltepe refugees will have to spend another harsh winter in tents.

The situation in the third camp, in Mus, where 6,800 Iraqi Kurds are confined, is even worse, according to Mr. Mayi. Police treat the refugees even worse than the police do in Kiziltepe. Only 50 to 60 refugees are permitted to leave the camp every day, and for only two hours. The people are very, very poor. They are not allowed to visit friends or relatives in the other two camps (Diyarbakir and Kiziltepe refugees can visit each other from time to time).

Mr. Mayi said that the Iraqi Kurds in all three camps have common concerns: first, all are concerned about their future. "For 20 months, the Turkish government has called us visitors to Turkey, not refugees." The United Nations High Commissioner for Refugees has

47

talked with the Turkish government about improving the lot of the refugees, but nothing has happened. "Our people are very sad," he said. "We are sure the Turkish government will not let us stay here, and we don't see any other place to go. The European countries have done nothing. We cry, and we write reports that we send to the UN, journalists and parliamentarians, and they say, 'yes, there will be a solution.' But we see nothing."

Second, the refugees are very concerned about having no schools for their children. Police tell them schools are not possible, because "you are not refugees, and you are not from Turkey." They believe their children are suffering permanent damage because of their lack of schooling.

Third, the refugees are very worried about their economic situation. The Turkish government has given them no money, and has not allowed other countries to help them, and most of them are not given an opportunity to work.

Mr. Mayi gave the Helsinki mission information on three episodes of alleged poisonings, one in each of the three camps. On June 8, 1989, 2,000 people were reportedly poisoned by bread in the Kiziltepe camp in Mardin. The poison affected the nervous systems of those affected; their bodies shook. No one died, but some people spent up to two months in the hospital.

Between one and two hundred people were poisoned in Mus camp in November 1989; again, it was traced to the bread.

On February 1, 1990, 1,700 people were poisoned by bread in the Diyarbakir camp. One hundred of them were seriously ill, with the same symptoms. Blood and bread samples were sent to a local laboratory for analysis, but the refugees never received any reports on the results.

Mr. Mayi says that the Iraqi Kurdish refugees are desperate about their situation: "All the world knows our situation, but no country does anything about it, because they are afraid of Turkey and Iraq's reactions, since they have economic relations with them. On the earth there is no other people in this condition. Where is the humanity? This is our only chance in life -- why is all the world silent?"

Recommendations

Helsinki Watch makes the following recommendations to the government of Turkey:

o   Rescind Decree 413 and restore the rights suspended by that decree;

o   Abolish the Village Guard system;

o   Protect the civilian population in areas where guerrilla warfare is taking place and comply with international laws governing internal armed conflicts;

o   End efforts to relocate civilians from troubled areas except in instances where their lives are endangered, and then only in accordance with Protocol II of the 1949 Geneva Conventions;

o   Refrain from using land mines, except in accordance with the provisions of international law;

o   Acknowledge the existence of the Kurdish minority and grant it the political and civil rights held by other Turks;

o   Permit lawyers to have immediate access to detainees and prisoners, including during the preliminary investigation; to speak Kurdish with prisoners; to meet with prisoners in privacy; to have adequate time to prepare cases; and to have access to all documents necessary to a prisoner's defense;

o   End restrictions that deprive Kurds of their ethnic identity: permit official use of the Kurdish language, music and dance and the celebration of Kurdish holidays; permit the use of Kurdish names;

o   Permit the establishment of Kurdish associations and
the publication of Kurdish books and periodicals;

o   Punish appropriately the abuse and humiliation of
civilians by security forces;

o   Acknowledge the pattern of torture in police detention
centers, take steps to end it, and increase sentences for
convicted torturers;

o   Prohibit the use in court of confessions obtained by
torture or coercion;

o   Amend the Penal Code to eliminate Articles 141, 142
163 and other Penal Code articles that are used to
deprive Turks of their human rights;

o   Stop all legal actions against the press and against
writers and publishers based on the content of their
writings, and release from prisons and detention
centers all those held for the expression of their
peaceful political views.

o   Grant refugee status to the Iraqi Kurdish refugees;

o   Improve living conditions in the refugee camps for the
Iraqi Kurds, including adequate housing for the
refugees now living in the Mardin camp;

o   Provide schools for the children of Iraqi Kurdish
refugees, or permit the Iraqi Kurds themselves to
educate their children.

Helsinki Watch recommends that the United States
Government:

o   condemn the human rights abuses detailed in this
newsletter and use its best efforts to persuade the
government of Turkey to carry out the
recommendations listed above; and

o   as required by Section 502B of the Foreign Assistance Act, state clearly what extraordinary circumstances warrant provision of military assistance to Turkey in light of its consistent pattern of gross violations of internationally-recognized human rights.

Previous Helsinki Watch Reports

Earlier reports on Turkey are available:

News from Turkey: Freedom of Expression. February 1990
News from Turkey: Eight Cases of Torture. July 1989.
Prison Conditions in Turkey. August 1989. 92 pages, $6.00.
Paying the Price: Freedom of Expression in Turkey. March 1989. 178 pages.
Destroying Ethnic Identity: The Kurds of Turkey. March 1988. 73 pages.
State of Flux: Human Rights in Turkey. December 1987. 159 pages.
Freedom and Fear: Human Rights in Turkey. March 1986. 122 pages.